Conten'

GW01048808

What is the wind?

The air around us moves. The wind is moving air. It has great power. We see it at work almost every day.

The wind moves around us with great power.

The wind is very powerful. We see this in storms. Look what the wind did to these trees in Britain in the Great Storm of 1987!

Some winds have the power to blow trees down.

Where does the wind blow?

We live in a sea of air that goes up to about 17 kilometres above us. There are no clouds above this height. There is no wind or weather above this height.

highest clouds – up to 17 kilometres

highest mountain – about 9 kilometres

The highest clouds are about 17 kilometres above Earth.

There is no weather above the highest clouds. There is no wind above these clouds.

The highest clouds above Earth have no weather above them.

Why does the wind move?

When air gets hot, it rises. Then cooler air comes in to take its place. The moving air is the wind. This is why it is windy near a big fire.

hot air rises

cooler air comes in as wind

It is windy near a big fire because the air is moving.

The sun heats the land. In hot places, the sun makes the land very hot. The very hot air rises and cooler air comes in. This cooler air is the wind.

hot sun

cooler air moves so the wind blows

hot air rises

hot land

cooler sea

Hot air rises from the hot land and cooler air comes in.

Wild winds in India

In India, the sun heats the land and makes it very hot in summer. The hot air rises and cooler wet air comes in from the sea. The wind brings rain and great storms called cyclones.

cooler air comes in from the sea

hot air rises

wind

In India, there are cyclones in the summer because the land is so hot.

The winds in the cyclones are wild. They have great power and bring too much rain. The rain makes the rivers too full of water. The water from the rivers floods the land. The floods kill many people every year.

Every year, many people are killed by the floods that come after the cyclones.

Wild winds in the Atlantic

The Atlantic is a big ocean between Europe and America. Many great storms start over the Atlantic. The sun heats up the water and great clouds are made. The clouds spin in the wind. These storms are very powerful. When a storm is very big it is called a hurricane. The middle of a hurricane is called the eye of the storm.

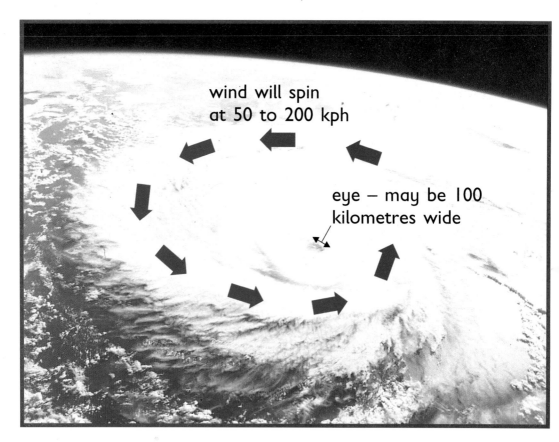

wind will spin at 50 to 200 kph

eye – may be 100 kilometres wide

The eye of a hurricane may be a hundred kilometres wide.

Hurricanes have great power. The hurricane wind spins very fast. Hurricanes can cause a lot of damage.

This damage was done by a bad hurricane in America.

Tornadoes

Some wild winds are not in big storms. Some winds spin and twist between the land and the clouds. These winds are called tornadoes. Tornadoes are not very wide but they are very powerful.

Tornadoes have a lot of power. They spin and twist between the land and the clouds.

Tornadoes rip up almost anything in their way. They can rip up houses, trees and cars.

Tornadoes can cause a lot of damage as they can rip up almost anything.

Why is it windy in cities?

Moving air in cities has to go around buildings. The air above the buildings does not have to go around anything. The air going around the buildings has to go further than the air going over the top. It has to go faster. This makes it windy.

wind here goes straight on

wind here has to go faster to get around

Moving air in cities has to go faster to get around buildings.

Wild mountains, wild winds

Moving air in the mountains has to go around the mountains. The air above the mountains does not have to go around anything. The air going around has to go further than the air going over the top. It has to go faster and this makes it windy.

wind here goes straight on

wind here has to go faster to get around

It can be very windy in the mountains.

Winds can cause danger on mountains in other ways. When wind goes over a mountain, it gets drier and warmer. If there is snow and ice on the other side of the mountain, it can melt. Then there is danger of an avalanche. An avalanche is a fall of rocks and melting snow and ice.

wind here gets drier and snow falls

wind here gets warmer and snow and ice melt

an avalanche of rocks and melting snow and ice falls down the mountain

Sometimes winds can cause an avalanche.

An avalanche can bring great danger. It moves very fast at about 200 kph. It is very powerful. Nothing can stop an avalanche and it can cause a lot of damage.

an avalanche can move at 200 kph

An avalanche moves fast at about 200 kph and can cause a lot of damage.

How the wind can help boats

There is no land all the way around the southern part of the world. There is no land to stop the wind so it blows fast. It blows right around the world from west to east all the time. Boats can sail very fast in the southern part of the world.

The wind blows fast in the southern part of the world.

It can be fun to sail boats in the southern part of the world. It can be fun but it can also be dangerous. The wind is wild.

Boats can sail fast but the sea and the wind are wild.

How the wind can help planes

The wind can also help planes. There is a wind that blows from west to east about 10 to 15 kilometres above Earth. It is called the jet stream. The jet stream moves very fast. It helps planes that fly from west to east to go fast.

The jet stream wind helps this jet to fly fast from west to east.

The jet stream moves at about 35 to 200 kph. The jet stream is caused by the spin of the planet Earth as it orbits the sun. The Earth spins from west to east.

Earth spins from west to east

The jet stream is caused by the west to east spin of the planet Earth.

How the wind makes power for us

We know that the wind has power. We know that the wind can move things. We have used the power of the wind in windmills for hundreds of years.

*Windmills have used the power of the wind
for hundreds of years.*

Now we have windmills that make electrical power for us.
Have you seen these types of windmills?

These new windmills make electrical power.

Glossary

Atlantic   an ocean between Europe and America

avalanche   a great fall of snow, ice and rocks

cooler   not as hot

cyclones   very windy storms that bring a lot of rain

drier   not as wet

tornadoes   winds that twist and spin

hurricanes   great windy storms that spin

slower   not as fast

warmer   not as cold